A Poet, On Park Hill?
Outside the Box
Full Colour Edition
By Rowan Blair Colver
All rights reserved © 2010, 2012

An Indigo Poet Creation

With thanks to Sandra Swan for her kind proof reading.

ISBN - 978-1480029361

To all those happy people doing the best they can

A Poet, On Park Hill?

By

Rowan Blair Colver

Outside The Box

2nd Edition

In a world of corruption
In a place I despise
In a social eruption
In a barrage of lies
In a frame of mind
In a place to find
In a zone I've become
In a tale of the one
In a book of old verse
In an alternate universe
In a dream dreamt out at sea
In a story all about me
In a song sung with tears
In a note you can't quite hear
In a place far from home
In an ocean all alone
I'm here

As you arrive in Sheffield UK by train from the South of England as many people do each day, if you just happen to gaze from a window, you are met with the view of Park Hill estate. It is easy to describe but difficult to fully appreciate until you actually see it, something which is going to be different very soon. A hill comes down from an area of nice looking terrace and detached houses and sprouting from the ground appears an oblong concrete slab. As the decline of the hill progresses into the valley which holds the train line, the concrete building does not. Instead it towers off into the sky reaching a huge degree of horizon blocking "there-ness". It has been standing there since the 1950's and has only really become grubbier and grubbier over those years. It was declared an area of architectural importance by the National Heritage Trust and has received a grade II status of listed building.

So it seems that Park Hill is here to stay, and unlike many of its cousins will not see the explosive experts and the huge jaws of demolition cranes...yet. No, as well publicised across the local and national news, Park Hill is being re-vamped and so far a small section has been completely gutted and has received brand new funky coloured panels. Most of the estate now is closed, and fenced off from the public.

However, on a secluded corner at the very top of the hill is a small area of flats which are occupied. This small haven within chaos is my home.

During the 1930's, the tight knit housing, steep dark gennels, wasteland and quarries of the Park area of Sheffield where the estate now stands was declared for renewal. The high levels of crime and population density had led to the area being termed "Little Chicago" by residents and neighbours. Like so many inner city hot spots, for this reason and others, it was decided by the housing authority that the back to back housing with shared plumbing was to be replaced.

A slow effort began to demolish and clear the buildings and wastelands, but when the Second World War began the project was put on hold. It was not until the 1950's when serious plans were formed to ensure the future of the area. In 1953 an architect from France called Le Corbusier inspired Ivor Smith, Frederick Nicklin and Jack Lynn. They mused and dreamt, and finally drew up the first plans for the "Streets in the Sky".

The Park Hill maisonettes, until very recently, remained mainly unchanged as they now stand sixty years into the future. In with the design came the ingenious use of the steep hillside, allowing most decks to be grounded further up the hill. This allowed motorized utilities such as milk floats and refuse collection to visit each resident in turn.

Water was provided to all maisonettes, along with sinks that had minor waste disposal systems in, feeding the scraps directly into the sewage pipe. This type of mechanism was known as the Garchey system. From 1957 to 1961 the work took place to build this recently termed "brutalist" structure.

The five streets, or rows, were named after some of the original road names that once stood in the area. These are Park Hill, Gilbert, Hague, Long Henry and Norwich. In total 995 maisonettes were built. They range from single person bedsits to family size three bedroom suites.

Because of the hillside, the estate ranges from four stories to thirteen stories as it progresses into the valley. Each home has two levels, some are up and some are down. The walls were bricked in orange, yellow and red which were built around concrete oblongs. These were then split into separate maisonettes with brick and plaster. The homes were soon filled with people from all across Sheffield. The old slum residents were first to be given homes, then other Sheffield dwellers.

After the blanket bombing endured by the city during the early to mid 1940s many people were in desperate need of a home. The rivers and hills provided easy landmarks for the Luftwaffe to locate and blitz this powerful and world famous source of metal and machine. The quick fix offered by this radical and new idea was the perfect opportunity for the city to give something back to its residents, who had worked so hard to protect the morale and esteem held within the structure of Sheffield.

In 1960, the first Christian Chaplain of Park Hill was registered. His name was Rev Brian Pallister Pritchard. He would be on hand to lend an ear or give advice to anyone who asked.

The official opening took place in 1961, which signalled the steady flow of new tenants into their brand new homes. During the 50s and 60s many immigrants came to Sheffield from Asia and the West Indies and many of these welcome newcomers also undoubtedly found themselves in places like this one.

Once and for all, Sheffielders could turn their back on low grade housing, no more cramming or queuing for the bathroom. The community spirit of yesteryear, empowered by the interwoven lives of so many was kept alive, even if only as a glimmer. The doors all open out onto wide, road like landings allowing people to walk outside and chat to each other, just like the old days.

The partially secluded walkways gave each section its own unique view of the estate, and each grew their own way of social converse, even if only slightly. However there was now space for play grounds, copses and lawns. People had room to breathe and much more privacy than before. The general unpleasantness of the slums was replaced with an easily sanitized living space. The surfaces are flat and square, the flats are all the same constructed with replaceable parts. If something needed cleaning or fixing it was done.

A team of workmen took residency here and only until recently did this continue. They come round every morning with litter picks and cleaning apparatus. They mop out the lifts and stairwells and collect bins on a daily basis. They cut the grass, tend the gardens and keep vermin at bay. People seemed to enjoy life on Park Hill, new homes, improved quality of life, and a sense that things were getting better. For twenty years the solution worked.

During the 1980s the cities major steel industry went into massive decline, and this lowered the average wage in Sheffield. The increase of poverty encouraged crime in poorer areas, like Park Hill. The right to buy scheme, which allows a council tenant to pay cut prices to own their rented home, meant that less desirable places like Park Hill became last resort housing. This double whammy of troubles resulted in a reputation for violence and crime. This reputation went on to encourage more crime, and people's attitudes began to change.

Sheffield, since this time, has been reborn as a business and information city, as well as supporting two major universities. Over a lengthy period in the mid 90's the maisonettes were refurbished with new kitchens and bathrooms and the clever sinks were replaced with less dangerous ordinary ones. The walls were all redecorated and the surrounding grounds got a well earned clean. The money seemed to have come back, and the people began to calm down. The reputation that Park Hill earned during its ten year dark age very slowly began to fade out along with the memories of steel.

As mentioned, in 1998 the National Heritage Trust declared Park Hill a building of architectural importance, and honoured it with a Grade II listing. This dashed the dreams of many people of Sheffield who wanted to see it ripped down and replaced with something more attractive. The copycat Kelvin flats, which were modelled upon the success of Park Hill, were demolished around this time.

So, during the 1990s, the estate became over run with every type of person possible. The shopping facilities enjoyed a good trade. A dentist, newsagent, pubs, co-op, travel agents, take aways, hair dressers, the list goes on. Also the primary school continued to run, educating the children who often had many language barriers and social backgrounds. It was at this point I moved in.

Over the next ten years things started closing down. Buildings became empty and slowly, during 2005, the rows began being fenced off. Demolition began soon after and within months huge sections of the estate were reduced to their concrete oblong boxes and mountains of rubble. Devoid of all brick work, plaster and memories, these cartons are to be redressed and given a fresh start. At the time of writing in 2010, the first replacement walls have been placed. Brightly coloured orange, red and yellow panels have been put up, mimicking the original brick work but in day-glow futuristic style. I think that probably sounds similar to what they said back in 1957!

Will anyone want to move in once it is revamped? Will anyone pay to own their flat? Urban Splash thinks so, as they hold the contract to renovate the entire estate. I wait with baited breath to see what happens to this place, my home.

When I first came to live in Sheffield back in 1995 I wondered what the people living up there on the flats were like. What was it like for them? What do they do? I was a naive teenager, but those were valid questions. Well, it wasn't before too long when I was moving out of home and registering for council housing. Low and behold, I was given a maisonette on the infamous Park Hill. Back then it was fully populated, and in fact the property I had then is now an empty shell awaiting new ceilings walls and windows. In those days, around 1999, every single maisonette was occupied, and most of the people were young, poor and without direction. Like me, a lot were depressed. Among the smart, self respecting ordinary folk were more than a fair share of people who yearned to be better.

Some had even forgotten about that, as their appearance was grubby and their speech was mumbled. Maybe it was just me, but I felt like this level of "lostness" appeared all too frequently around here. Especially in the beginning, when I moved in here, back in 1999. There were notable levels of crime too, on several occasions I was offered drugs ranging from fake cannabis to very real heroin.

I witnessed a stabbing and simultaneously witnessed people simply walking by without phoning for help. I had no phone but informed the shop who said "an ambulance will be coming, someone will ring one". So that's it. No-one rushed to his aid, and no-one in the shop rushed to a phone. Not knowing what else to do, I ashamedly just went home. After informing the shop, I felt I could do no more.

My first flat was one of the biggest Park Hill has to offer. A kitchen and living room was downstairs, then upstairs to three bedrooms, a bathroom and separate toilet. I shared this with two friends, I went to work while they did what they did, I went out a lot and it was fun. It wasn't much of a home, more like a place to sleep. I had so many visitors to that place. I remember my friends returning home with a whole troop of followers, taggers on, who wanted somewhere to sit and be warm. Somewhere that wasn't their home. I think the intrigue of the looming flats over town had lured them in, and when offered a place to sit within the forbidden walls, they could not refuse.

I soon found myself in another flat, a tiny bedsit at the top of the hill. It was right next door to a makeshift police station. The police sign had been defaced to read "lice", and then someone badly replaced the missing letters with white paint. Often I'd see them coming and going, sometimes they had someone in cuffs. One time I saw a whole patrol of police marching one man to a car. He must have done something pretty bad. I have often seen members of emergency services referring to maps of the estate with door numbers added to them. This is not something that is widely available and must have been especially provided for them. If you don't know your way around it is very easy to go round in circles.

For a small time I had three other adults with their dog living within the two rooms that was my home. This was fun at times; we would never have a boring night. Cabin fever does affect you, and best friends have to sometimes put differences aside when sharing living space. The kitchen had a double bed in it, and my living room had a double bed in it as well. The hall way was home to a computer on a tiny desk with a swivel chair. Everything else was crammed into any spare bit of space I could find.
I had a neighbour at this second maisonette who was absolutely crazy. He would falsely accuse me of hammering on the floor all night and shouting, he would accuse me of taking heroin and he even offered me help from a methadone clinic. This man also attempted to scare me with threats of violence, swinging fists and foul language. But in my typical style I did not back down and much to my relief no fists were raised by me.

So on from there, I moved across the estate to my current maisonette where I am at the time of writing in 2010. We are the last people now on here until it is regenerated and the whole new flux of residents move in to the shiny new Park Hill. So what of those questions, what is it like on Park Hill, who lives there? What are they like?

Well after eleven years I think I qualify as someone, and one of the last, one of the very last. I just happen to be a poet and a writer, so I thought I'd compile this book using some of the poetry written by myself in the years I have been here. I have battled with depression, and felt the waves of paranoia and isolation, but I have also had some of the most exciting and brilliant times of my life.
A lot of people will pretend to be sincere and friendly, but they just take all they can. These are everywhere, but personally I feel I have handled my fair share. This short poem is a comical reminder on trust.

He went to town with a million quid
In just one place he'd spend most of it
No material did he purchase
But in heaven he owns a space, he gave it to God
Now the preacher in his sports car
Driving to the boat club
On an island in the ocean a thousand miles away

Some people would come to your door in the company of friends that you know in a roundabout way and often they would be great, a little shy about being on such a scary looking block of flats, but mainly they are ok. A lot of good people have been introduced to me by being taken to my home. I think at some point in the past I was a popular venue for people. I always had tea or coffee, biscuits, and music on offer. However you get the odd one. You know the types of folk who loiter around city centres with sob stories about this that and the other, and after a very long speech they ask for money? Well sometimes it's one of these types who end up on the sofa drinking your tea. Sometimes they don't seem to have the tell tale signs, their clothes are nice, they appear polite, they may even be generous towards you the first few times. However, these certain types would always end up wanting more than they should do. They tend to ask for too much in too little a time. Endless nights on the armchair, the coffee jar is mysteriously empty, things like that. Even money has gone missing when in the company of new friends. It doesn't take many times of this to get used to kindly asking people to leave.

There are plans inside plans
Dark subconscious smiling conscious
I know what they are
No real originality met
Just existing scarring the seal
I know where they are
Afloat still sinking a perfect irony
Such tiny seeds weigh as selfish irony
Hollow yet dense the paradox shatter
All is clear now yet it shouldn't matter
Nothing is an illusion
No-one likes pollution
Gone is the confusion
Here is the solution
Strike the filth with smite
Tear out pages of lies
Cast aside falsely acquired warmth
Stand alone in an empty cold world

Recently, there has been a large increase in outside attention towards these flats. The reason I started this book was to give an insider's account. So many have come from their homes to visit mine, and then write about it, or tell stories. Sometimes it feels a bit like a zoo for the posh. We had this music event once for a local record label. This sounded good and I particularly was looking forward to it. But when it happened the area got fenced and tickets were very expensive. Many security guards turned up to protect the public from goodness knows what and we were forced to stand well back out of the way. People were not allowed to access vital walkways for a safe and well lit route through to their own home. Television programs have been made here too.

Once I opened my front door to find a man who I know from TV giving a monologue to a camera about how people want better than this. It was bang outside my door. Of all the doors! For a few minutes I spied on him through my peep hole, something that a lot of doors have on here. He was very animated, and sounded passionate about it. He wasn't going to stop me from going to the shop though. As I opened my door and stepped outside, the presenter and the camera man stopped and looked. "Sorry" I said, "Oh no, it's quite alright" he replied. There was a look in his eyes but I can't describe it. Maybe it was surprise, yes, I think it was. Perhaps he thought I'd look different somehow. And I'm sure he got his scene, eventually.

A lot of people on these flats have what is called an electric key meter. Because of low income the power companies prefer to tie you to these devices which allow you to put on the energy money each week from your earnings.

The rates at which energy is charged are higher than a normal meter, but people with less money pay for their liability. They also control how much you pay for any arrears you may have. Typically it is around £9 per week on top of what you consume, which is a large fraction of many people's income. It is more than how much a lot of people use in their week meaning they pay over double on already inflated rates. It goes towards debt but it is unaffordable to people who normally do struggle. This is a poem written about the times when the power goes and the money doesn't come until tomorrow, or later, and it's time to get the candles lit.

Take a turn to the dusty road
And wander past its doors
Minds with plans they call
this home
With coloured walls and fires
warm
Dreaming heads of people lay
Upon pillow with blanket
wrapped
Troubled minds of some just
sit
And gaze beyond the feelings
trapped
Only once the candles are lit
Can we put a stop to this
Down into tombs say the
weak and the fools
With cries of the sky and talk
of the moon
All falls on the shoulders of
men
Blaming the rain

The clouds and its shame
Not the idolatry that caused
the mistake
For heaven's sake
Only once the candles are lit
Can we put a stop to this
Killing the lie is all lullaby
when it's televised
And written down by the
editors crown
And twisted and ground
down
To become food for the fire
flies
Who light the way to fear and
woe
Down that well lit sanitized
road
Where your posters feed more
lies to our minds
Only once the candles are lit
Can we put a stop to this

In my current home I have a balcony, or veranda, as they are commonly called. Some are outdoor junk rooms, some are where the dog sleeps and some are beautifully decorated, lush spaces. Mine is covered in plant pots each attempting to sustain their own item(s), shrub, herb or bush. I have had so many countless plants, and many of them do not survive.

The red brick work has remnants of graffiti left by previous residents. Even various nooks and crannies indoors contain written effigies to someone or other. Most have been painted over during the several redecorations which I have undertaken. Outside my veranda is a car park, then a road, then a grassy hill which flows right down to the station. Then beyond is the valley, and far off into the distance are the slopes of a few of Sheffield's six other hills, making seven in total. I get a direct wind most days which completely obliterates many plants I try to grow; only the hardiest survive.

So what plants I do have I really adore, as they have battled snow and icy winter winds. Plus the drenching evening sun which sets into the city centre which is directly West from my point. At night the moon will sometimes come right across my view and hang in the air all night, and a few particularly vivid stars still manage to peek through the copious lighting of Sheffield centre at night. The colours of the sky are quite literally awe inspiring and jaw dropping. So many words have been written about the things I see from my veranda. Here are a few.

The moon it sings to the shyest stars
It's voice it flows that far
Its barren canyons resonate low
And to the valleys and hills below
Where we're going or where we're from
All distant memory from time long gone
Seeking my fortune through time and space
A different galaxy a different place
Violet skies with glowing eyes
A mystery to behold
Nightmares die as I stumble and find
A treasure for me to hold
As I travel far and wide it seems
I've been here before in a dream
Luring me to this spinning blue rock
Our fortunes dictated my destiny locked

A world from tomorrow's eyes there will always be enough
No one will go without when we all know how to love
Purposes of life inside when their voices become ours
Each will find and unfold a hundred little flowers
Chainmail of cosmic magnitude
Embrace my vulnerability
Years of near perfect solitude
Disgrace my personality no more

We look up to the stars our cup they always fill
Vexatious minds are nulled our senses change their will
Look far inside yourself what jewels can you see
Shining in the cold black space where your money used to be

All the time for this can become a single moment
Purest hearts will miss an age still lying dormant
A world of light and love for us all, believing in the one who will
not let us fall too far

How I yearn for a garden
My flesh and sap is craving a bed
A red pot a green pot and blue
No match for what
Can be found in the earth
To be rained on not watered
To be sunny all day long
And to be dark at night
Without the living room lights on

The thing about living so high up, in the highest story flats, which are now gutted and hollow, the view was phenomenal. Because from the window the land slopes down into the valley, which then has the adjoining flood plain, you can see for miles. A keen eye can spot the woods around Forge Dam, the woods at Rivelin and the ones around Firth Park. Beyond these are rolling green spaces, grass land and fields. On a not so clear day the actual horizon is so obscured by the atmosphere that it looks like it could go on forever.

Up here there is no horizon
Up here nothing is surprising
Fired up beyond the sky
Distant gravity to say we can't
cry
Silent explosions fill our view
We are the chosen lucky few
Allowed to sit and fantasize
All you do is close your eyes

And you're there
Spiraling dancing
Circling prancing
The gift to see beyond
A forever out the window
Up here there are no shadows
Just leave it up to chance
To a gateway for the stars

Because the train line runs so close to our home it is very usual to hear the sound of a train coming in or pulling away. The loud speakers can sometimes be heard if the wind permits, slurred place names and times bouncing in the air around the windows. Late at night freight trains sometime come and move slowly through the station without actually stopping. As they slow right down their brakes will squeal as they creep past in the night. The sound of heavy duty steel and iron crawling across the track is a haunting one and the size of these trains really draws out the noise.

Awake to the time table
Old train rattles by
Alone on the turntable
Out here I will try
Rusty tracks sleepers amiss
Gears jammed through time
I would call home to assist
But someone cut the line
Only choice but to push
Direct the rails by force
Just stay awake don't rush
It's all part of the course
Trains at low speed in chaos
No direction at all
How soon before the loss
Of the drivers control

Trains aren't the only thing that can be heard from up here. On a football day it is not uncommon to hear thousands of Blades singing praises to their beloved Sheffield United. Copious roars of approval hurl across the hill as goals are scored. On weekend nights the sound of parties sometimes are carried up here too; wailing people having drunken fun, singing, shouting and general noise. When things turn sour, as they often do; the angry shouts of men suddenly overpower the women's jollity for a moment or two, then normally this subsides back to the sound of enjoyment. If any events occur in the city centre then we get to hear them, even if only slightly. A heavy metal concert was staged in the stations outdoor concourse. It was so loud that we could hear it properly, almost note for note. As the crow flies it is maybe up to half a kilometre away.

The residents on Park Hill have always been so down to earth and realistic. We as a whole don't really care for all the trimmings that go with living somewhere with more expensive homes. That's not to say we are a bunch of scrubbers, far from it. We take pride in ourselves and our actions. An example of this local sense of pride can be seen in something as simple as a flower bed. The residents who live next to a certain raised bed have populated it with bulbs and shrubs. Years later, they still grow healthy and tall. Now, if the kids and youths were half as bad as what people say they are, why is that flower bed supporting life? Why isn't it ripped up, trampled and burnt? Because everyone cares. From the OAPs to the angry teenager, this place is respected, its people are respected and that's how we like it. It led me to write this when I decided to complain about certain types of people who will ignorantly go about their lives without thinking about the things that really matter.

Look at you with your hair
and your suit
Your millimetre stubble and
designer label shoes
Look at you with your nine
eleven and a half
Your golden signets and
taffeta twisted scarf

Once newborn and covered in
slime
The only vocabulary a throaty
stuttered whine
But now a big shot high flight
icon of career
Silver lining from selling the
poor gassy beer

Now, let me be honest. I spent a lot of time in my younger days feeling very depressed, low and deep in thought. Repetitive cycles constantly plagued my brain and I became more and more detached. Or was that really true? Actually, what was happening was I was waking up. Seeing things as they really are, and deciphering them into feelings of tension and negativity. The ghosts of the area plagued my imagination, seeping their thoughts into mine. The world I was part of was in pain, all the greed and one-upmanship happening every day. So much selfishness and blind money grabbing is always going on without a care for anyone apart from those who have the big money on offer. People are made to feel certain ways about certain things and turn a blind eye to the fact that the system they happily follow is pushing people down.

Like shadows into reflective
skin
To ease your sleep take away
the pain
And dream of flowers
growing again
Ethereal existence of an
elemental entity
Multicarnate monster of your
dream
The faces of my reason it
seems
The faces of my reason
Multi dimensional universe
And a three dimensional
mind

Something is a little perverse
When other directions we find
It seems to be from long ago
Little things all the extra
things
Now become hesitant to show
Reluctant to reveal songs they
sing
Crystal gazing entities yonder
Horizons shifting in the sky
Place to place footprints
wander
Yet no-one sees who asks
them why

As I mentioned earlier, there was a man who would come from next door and accuse me of shouting and hammering on the floor. The apparent noise would often be around times I wasn't in, or in bed. What it could have been was a friend knocking on my door rather persistently but more than likely it was a fabrication made to excuse a confrontation. This was a common occurrence and many an evening was spent either panicking because he had said something, or feeling angry and ready to kick his door in. I never really did anything about it apart from argue with him, not even a complaint to the council, something which I actually should have done. I wrote this at the time...

If I could find the words
I'd mention how I feel right now
If this was the second verse
I'd start to show you how
But seeing as there is no time
Our world is spinning in pantomime
And things are never what they seem
Have you seen this one before?
With the old man wrapping on your door
Banging the woodwork hard
Alerting you of the thoughts he had
About how your voice is louder, louder than it is

This individual doesn't deserve mentioning any further, but I wish to add this. It has been 8 years since I first encountered this man, and only the other day he confronted me in the city centre and began spouting the usual nonsense abuse at me. C'mon man, get a life.

When I first get a maisonette on Park Hill, and there have been three in total that were mine, I have always been faced with a disgusting empty box filthy with stains, mould and old chipped paint. When it comes to decorating, the walls are so thin that if you knock a nail in for anything at all you are likely to hear the crumbling and dropping of shoddy plastering behind the paint. Any item with weight cannot really be put on the wall, as over time it will slide off. The heating is called "district heating". This means that when you pay the rent a fraction goes to the council department who provide the hot water for the taps and radiators. The heat is provided by burning the city's waste in a big incinerator just down the road. The chimney doesn't have any visible emissions on most days, and it doesn't smell. My home is always either freezing cold or roasting hot. It often smells dusty after putting the radiators on in a new flat, and on one occasion it was particularly bad. A window had been left open and a pigeon had been the squatting tenant. Luckily I managed to evict the creature without a fight as my towering form was enough to make it fly away. In my bedsit, that was my second maisonette, I found several needles lying about the place which the council should really have cleaned up, and I also found loads of fag buts and grime. I can only imagine what kind of nightmare place it used to be before I got it, and what sort of hell the poor neighbour had to endure as well. No wonder he was so unpleasant towards me!

In this place
A room cold and decayed
Set in face
A mournful look now frayed
Pray for a beacon
Pray for redemption
On hard stone our knees
Cold and decayed our plea
I saw a face
I felt the burning of spent
ember
A desolate place
I saw what I remembered
Spanning the empty more
emptiness like wind

Replacing nothing with a
negative non space
Everything slow as the
corners are trimmed
Nothing now with nowhere to
be displaced
No doctor
No medical examination
Just a square wheel on a circle
road
There is nowhere to go
Only the waste belongs
Only a long time ago
When no-one knew of their
place

Bringing the mood back again to the veranda, looking out at night over the city I see houses with lights out in every direction. I wonder about who is behind each window, their mood, their plans, what they have been doing. Then beyond lie the fields of green with hedges and forests. I imagine walking the wooded paths at night, the sounds and smells, the atmosphere of such a dark and seemingly distant place. I often see cars parking up in the quiet cul-de-sac which is outside my living room window. I don't know what goes on in the darkened windows and I don't really look. Sometimes two cars pull up within a few minutes of each other, and people get into other cars and so forth.

There was one time, in the day, when a barbecue on an upstairs veranda had summoned the attention of the fire brigade. The black plastic smoke coming from whatever packaging they had decided to burn was probably the dominant factor. Of course when the firemen, with suits and breathing gear, found it to be a barbecue they went back. However, a statutory police car also turned up which then decided to take a look at a conspicuous Jag parked up on the side. Suits and sniffer dogs later, a man was cuffed and the car was towed away. I can only assume drugs were involved. The constant lighting in my inner city location means that song birds chirrup all day and night. It is not uncommon to catch a few notes, late at night, from a bird singing in a nearby tree or from a wall or lamp post.

The city lights come
streaming in
Through winter trees with
branches thin
Ochre leaves will twist then
spin
As they float through the
whispering wind
The dreaming Earth
gracefully turns
As wet frost hangs from the
ferns
One more journey comes to
adjourn
What have we done, seen and
learned
Cob webs cast with glistening
dew
Rising sun the day is already
new
Meek dawn chorus the birds
now few

Slow hours past sat waiting
for you
Nostalgia rife as wood smoke
drifts
Chimney leaning giving
diagonal lift
Through picture turn and
memory sift
A distant day when winter
lovers kissed
As the waning sunlight
trickles over the windswept
moors
As the nightjar stirs ready to
sing until dawn
I silently wander on into the
fog beyond
Where our dreams are said to
be found

At some points the depression becomes very difficult to manage. I was undoubtedly irritating towards all my friends during the difficult times in the past. Now as a more mature adult than before I like to think when I'm going through turmoil within I can close it off to those who don't need to know. But this has not always been the case. Many a lip sucking memory causes that lemon juice effect in my mouth, but more in my tummy....if you know what I mean.

Egoless humanoid aimlessly
falls apart
Senseless sensual entity
becomes noir art
Collapsing lifespan crushing
onlookers so run
You don't want this, my life is
done

Salt in the wound you're
happy that's enough
Who cares about my mind
and all that stuff?
No-one but me don't you see
How can I believe in someone
who doesn't exist?
Can you do the same?

Well that is all very dramatic but I'm not trying to make you feel sad. I will keep the depressing poems to the bare minimum, but it does reflect a style I adopted for many years. I think it must have helped me to vent how I felt without causing offense. I have a spiritual outlook on my mind these days and my poetry reflects this. The beginning of this change was very subtle and perhaps occurred years before even I noticed it. But here is a poem written at the same time as the last one.

Celebration of light eternal
Material entity of infinite
depth
Unless we negatively dwell
Tell of those whose hearts are
pure
Lured into a dream of light
Flight of cleansed being so
soar

More still the elation will stir
Preferred by universal
thoughts
Short are the days long are the
nights
But never too far from golden
light

Once I was invited to someone's home who lived only round the corner and up the stairs. Before this point the only flats I had been in were those I rented and those of other young people. They were all scruffy, untidy and dirty from even before we had moved in. This one however was pristine, the walls were clean and nicely decorated, the things were all shiny and new looking and a lot of things were there that looked expensive. I was ashamed. I had been led into this self taught thinking that people living here couldn't make a home like this. But I was wrong. I took steps then on to improve my home and now it's even better than the one that inspired me!

One day I will be there
The wind blowing through
my hair
Alongside the others no joke
Watching all the lonely ones
choke
I have no crystal ball
Cannot predict anything at all

But watching knowing the
rest
It doesn't end just yet
Now is not tomorrow
Who knows if there is sorrow?
Can it be it never turns?
Will you stay or will you
learn?

Farewell sweet childhood the memory serves me well,
A future of self taught depth to find stories to tell
Where is the flaming one what has become
Of the whisperer of the mountain sun
Trampled underfoot are the remains of shattered hope and dreams
In a ditch of disaster is what it all seems
How far does this disillusion reach its stench, its screech?
Knee deep I wade toward the barren beach
Wooden raft nestled in the lee of a soul claiming rock
Tied to a hook with a simple merchant knot
Unleashed my vessel groans as the wind takes grip
Onto the skyline awaits my gleaming ship

It wasn't long before I had made friends on many corners and rows of the estate and I would spend a lot of my spare time visiting these people. It is great to think that although the social problems were blatant, many people would still keep their doors unlocked. I guess the attitude is that "fear ye all who enter without nice intentions". Would you walk uninvited into a stranger's home in a place like Park Hill? The thing about the layout is that on paper it looks quite simple but when you are actually walking around it, it becomes a maze. So many people have told me about how they got lost on my flats. I have been lost too, when I first arrived.

At the end of a knotted length of string
What have I missed will I ever win?
How many weaves and twists confuse me?
Shout pulling trying to force uniformity
Hopeless at giving up hope for a hopeless cause
Every corridor has an open door
All these keys fit all but one
All these doors lead all but in

When deciding to leave the home at night it was sometimes a huge ordeal. A sufferer of anxiety would tell you that going outside is tricky, so imagine a sufferer of anxiety at night on Park Hill. I would need to psyche myself up to do things like visit the Park Hill Balti, which was a take away selling curried dog food on "The Pavement" the old shopping concourse, now reduced to rubble.

The modern rubbish disposal system on Park Hill is fairly simple. You are provided with three black sacks on a Tuesday at around 4pm. These are to be filled and left outside at 8am (Monday – Friday) for collection. At some random point in the morning the green suited workmen will drive past in their bright orange electric cars and pick up the bags. People who do not follow this routine, and leave their bins out whenever they like, are subject to letters about possible fines. We all get them, from time to time, when lots of people start forgetting the rules. Different landings have different ethics to bins. On some landings they pile them all up in an end corner, and some outside the front doors. If you can't wait until the next morning and want to dispose of a bin during the day, a lot of people will leave it outside someone else's door to avoid being frowned upon themselves. Or, you can throw it out the window. I have seen parked cars with exploded rubbish bags all over them. Nice! A lot of furniture and things get left out too. Complete living room set ups, wardrobes, tables and chairs- you name it, it gets left out for the bins. Like many before and many after, I have furnished several rooms by recycling this stuff. I would wander around late at night, looking for something to have for my home. It was quite fun, like shopping without money. Sometimes I would go home empty handed, but often I would not. Another thing that I would do, when it was late, was to take the short walk into the city centre. Around 4am the delivery came for a chain of bakeries. Waste trolleys full of bread, cakes and buns were wheeled out for disposal. With permission, a friend and I would fill carrier bags full of this stuff for the cupboards. This happened regularly for a while, but that particular driver moved on and his replacement would rather see the food dumped.

I can re-use yesterday's news
Now the olds but no worse
than cold
As it was left outside again
So to pull and to yank
This bundle of planks
And screws with bits that

wobble and flap
It's a hundred yards to my
front door
Round that bend and push
some more
This beauty's coming home
with me!

Crumbs of time scattered upon the floor
Production line of spirits to end the war
Severed bonds re-aligned unto the Sun
Do you understand what has just begun?

Five sided entity
Beams of light
In this crystal light we fly
Deep seated empathy
Candle flame
Memories the same but no more pain
Tonight.

Like many young people living on the flats when they were fully open I felt I had no real voice. My entire life seemed to be dictated by a higher authority. Suits and thugs alike, it was like I had to watch my every move. Every week I would pay my rent and do the shopping and go back to my little concrete box and sit with my things wondering what it must be like for everybody else. I had no self esteem to think I could be successful at anything, and so they kept me squished down, deciding when I got paid and how much, when I went to town and when I went without.

For quite a few months I was living on less than fifty pounds per fortnight. The government tell you to eat five portions of fruit and veg a day, and on the money they decided I had to live on, I hardly had enough for one portion a day.

Greet the times with an open
armed smile
Or the times will suspect you
know too much
See the suit as the pillar you
do not dispute
Or the suit will fold over your
life forever
Message from the microwaves

A symbol in the sky
The beginning of the universe
Was really when it died
Our ghost world sinks into
self infliction
The exploding sky outward
and beyond
A paradox of definition
Why we sing a mournful song

A lot of the people here are very hard working, and keep their thoughts clean and to themselves. Around 8am I see dozens and dozens of smartly dressed people walking into town for their jobs. But when there are a lot of young people in similar situations living close to each other, for someone who has sensitivities to atmosphere and social mood it is easy to be drawn backwards although you do your best to stay above water. It's all too easy to fall into the trap of believing it's ok to be going nowhere, it's ok to have little hope or self esteem.

Nothing isn't something you
can hold in your hands
Nothing isn't something that
dreams can understand
Nothing isn't something we
can all do without
So nothing isn't nothing after
all, there is a reason for
prejudice
When there's a reason to
compare
There's a reason to be proud
of this, when it's going round
your head
And the day is here when
beyond the fear
Lays a river to cleanse your
dreams
And the time has come when
things are done
With perfect reason in mind
Yet spiteful words from
nowhere spring

And thorned thoughts start
dragging me in
Building weight to pull me
down
Drawing a raincloud, casting
a frown
Not quite awake, too late to
sleep, these memories still real
Quivering hands hide my
eyes, the morning sun
screams
Not content with the breeze,
I'm still inside
Not decided to go out today
What kind of life, shallow
breathing
Light still screaming in, why
is this not a dream?
A waking world re-kindles
And my tired eyes close, this
light doesn't stir me
Why is this not a dream

Ask anybody that has lived here and kept food in their home, which is almost every single person, and they will tell you about the ants. Pharaoh's ants to be precise; a tropical variety that thrives in warm conditions. The permanent heating of the estate is therefore ideal. They follow chemical trails along walls and corners, searching for protein and sugar. Any meat or spreads or anything like that is subject to infestation. I have found several huge nests in my home from time to time as I track down the source of the trails. The ants don't bite and they don't sting. But what they do is get everywhere. The number of packets and jars I have had to throw away is unbelievable. Once I even poured out some cereal and found what looked like thousands of ants in my bowl. I try to keep foods at risk in the fridge which has the magnetic door. This is the only really safe place. People ask me why the bread is in the fridge, why the cereal and fruit is in there, I say "ants". The only real option is to get the exterminator in which is expensive and only gets rid of them for a short period if at all. It has been free in times past but not anymore. Another way is to leave all the heating off for about three or four days during mid-winter. I have had to do this second method a number of times but it does work. Going on a short holiday does the job. I once looked up the bait online and it comes from the USA in bulk. The website reported customs difficulties in getting the chemicals to members of the general public, so really I was stuck into paying for a professional, which I couldn't really do at the time.

This parasitic paradise, for a pestilence of legs
Crawling in the kitchen shade
And carpet creeping underlay
With baited lips I await their flavour
As darkened snacking I savour
Without checking first for ants

Ants aren't the only wildlife around here. The city centre/valley scenario provides a slightly warmer ambient temperature than further away, and in combination with the many areas of green space dotted around we have a large array of local flora and fauna. I have seen foxes and rats which are found in many places like this, but there are also hedgehogs, voles, kestrels, jays, yellow hammers, blue butterflies and lots more. Just the other day I found a piece of wood that had about 50 ladybirds on it, and in these were at least 6 different species. Some were with spots, some with blotches, and some with yellow shells, some black and some red, big and small. We have a family of mallards living on the metal sheds outside my veranda. They often quack to each other at random intervals. This is their third year of residency. I wonder if it's the same two ducks each time. Once I did worry because I found the decapitated head of a male mallard on the grass out the back. This wasn't our mallard though as I had the relief of seeing it sitting there when I got home. I found a friendly red and black moth once called a Burton. Apparently this is a rare insect! I have been honoured with the majesty of seeing a kestrel catch, kill and eat a prey. I witnessed its trademark hover, and then it suddenly darted downwards. A moment later it re-emerged with a writhing beast in its talons. A few squeezes later and it stopped its movements, then the kestrel landed and ate its meal.

A soaring bird can sometimes be heard
By its cry intent and shrill
Some distant thing on tilted wing
Still circles on high until
A movement minute then a downward swoop
The silence creeps in like a thief
The stolen sound and approaching ground
Then a panic cut short beneath

I would get all sorts of people knocking on my door, wanting my time. From salesmen to debt collectors for previous tenants, happy shoppers (shop lifters) selling from bin bags to religious types preaching their version of events. It was on one of these occasions that some right wing Christian disciples came to my door. I would talk to them about God, about how I believed in the same God as them, but so does everyone who has a faith; it doesn't matter to me what your name for God is, if that being is responsible for your life and the life of creation then that's all that matters. If you disagree, that's fine. Well they kept coming back, persistent bunch. They said to me that I was actually going to die and never return because I had friends that were non believers, they said I couldn't do things unless God specifically said I could. So no football then or catching a bus at that, not that I could pay the fare- it's cheaper to park a car than take the family by bus. Anyway, I digress, these people then said they want to take me to their place of worship, but they are not allowed to come to the door for this one, I have to meet them at a certain time outside. I didn't bother.

Battling demons all day, sleeping with angels at night
Living gargoyles are my prey
Will you join me in the fight?
I'm a spiritual warrior
Make the world a better place
With my ancient fiery sword
I cut down the non believers
And justly spreading the word
Make sure you can hear us

As the name suggests, we live on a hill. It is incredibly steep in a few places. The main way onto the estate from town is up the hill. There are three main routes. You can follow the tram line, and then walk up past the scented lilacs and poppies, and up the main front of the building. Or you can go through the station and up a very steep cobbled path. The cobbles here are used from the old roads which used to be where the flats are now. The third way is to go right up round the back and enter the estate from its highest point. There is however a fourth way. Just across from the station is an unlit and enclosed metal tunnel. In the dark this is very menacing. Its walls are drenched in graffiti and urine. Its floor is sprinkled with fag packets, empty cans and sweet wrappers. The odd needle packet or swab can also sometimes be seen. Once this passage has been walked through you will come out onto the tram line. Beyond this is an extremely steep cobbled hill, nick named "heart attack hill". It is steeper than any road for a car and has a rusty metal banister on one side. In the snow this can be a bit slippy as I, and many others have discovered.

It seemed to me in the early days, when I was a newcomer to the estate that the childhood fantasy that I had carried with me and drawn strength from was missing from so many people. They seemed dull, so down to earth it was actually a bad thing. When someone is being so real it becomes unreal then problems arise. That is why a good imagination and the confidence to express it is, in my humble opinion, a great thing for a youth.

Where's that guy with the magic carpet?
A linear device with swirls
Who's that boy with the real machete?
That thinks he's won the girls
What happened to enthusiasm?
Of a child out late at night
When is it all going to make any sense?
Won't you please shed some light?

To get to higher levels of the flats, to the "Streets in the Sky" you could take a long and breath taking climb up the bright blue spiral metal steps of doom, (known for jumpers and fitness freaks) or you can take the lift, or as some people like to call it, the public toilet. Yes folks, for some reason unknown to all you ask they have nearly always become the container for a puddle of urine, and sometimes worse. The buttons for the floor selection have often become stained with phlegm and it is advisable to use your door key to press them. The tall blue staircase is now gone, as are the flats which they led to. Only their skeleton remains for the time being. Once I called a lift from a high floor and when it finally arrived there was a raging fire inside. The flames leapt out at me from inside their previous confinement and I was forced to jump backwards. Some rather suspicious looking kids lurking round the corner in the stairwell repeated my frantic curses as I counted my blessings I hadn't been closer. So, when I finally do catch a lift, one that is clean and safe, the next worse thing is that someone gets in that you don't really trust. Being locked in a small box with a thug or a madman isn't very nice. Unfortunately it happened to me several times, and once or twice I came out poorer or in a less happy mood than before I entered.

Crocodile smiling don't trust me
I'll ruin your week wait and see
Run now
Get away
I'm bad news please believe
A slippery slope
Demise from the state of non upset
Warn you
Don't trust me
If you don't believe you've not met me yet

These concrete streets that's
what they're for
To drag my heart from door
to door
Like Godzilla is a metaphor
For when the buildings all fall
down
These fleeting things they
come and go
With haste they turn and let
you know
I can't see through this
window
When grime it sticks like
mildew to the glass
Oh it's part of the furniture
This thing that we are going
through

It's part of the furniture
And this is helping you to
learn
Sampling thought from others
minds
Opening doors to see what's
inside
Are you scared of what you
might find?
Or do you know nothing
hurts your life
Shaded glade where lights can
dance
This river it deserves a second
chance
Wash away the poisoned
land; give some time for the
system to renew

We have lost most of the major conveniences of yester years; however a few shops are on Duke Street which is a major feeder road for the city centre. They are only a two minute walk away and I often visit and pay the famously over-the-odds prices they ask for various essential goods. I saw a woman do a big shop in there once and maybe got in two days food but spent what I would usually spend on a week for my whole family! One of the times I had decided to take the short walk to go and buy something or other I opened my front door to see several men wearing all black and wearing balaclavas. One was right outside my door. I noticed the word "police" in tiny writing on the sleeve and breast but you really had to stare. He gave me a gruff look with angry eyes, the only thing visible through his attire. I smiled at him, nodded and he just continued to look angry. So, I shut my door.

The next day one of the neighbour's doors was missing, when I saw the person in question a few days later they reported "naw't 'appened" which to those who have not had the pleasure of knowing Yorkshire means "nothing happened". I had some brilliant parties. Sometimes there have been so many people crammed in my flat that there hasn't been room to move. It's amazing what free booze can do to a circle of friends. They all come out the woodwork, people who would previously never step foot in the area suddenly pull up in taxis and request a personal escort to your door. Occasions where the bath tub has been full of beers and wine, every room fully populated with people, music blasting from several stereos.

To be honest I have forgotten many of their faces, and their personalities. I can remember complete strangers arriving in droves in the company of one person I knew. Until fairly recently, this happened a lot in all three of my flats on here. We would have Nintendo tournaments, winner stays on. The game of choice was usually killer instinct, or street fighter 2. We would sit and have deep conversations about the nature of reality, the concept of religion and the meaning of problems. We must have solved world hunger and created world peace a dozen times within my walls, only by the morning the plans are long forgotten. I know a lot of musicians and nights have been spent all sat around with instruments making random improvised music for hours all night long. I have made some amazing friends through these things, and my memories serve me very well indeed.

Smokey room candle lit show
Sax playing jazzman keepin' it slow
Wine waiter scurries tables lay in queue
Keep it at head chill perhaps minus two
Laid back puffing
There isn't anything to get in the way
Stylish and sweet this goes on till late
Round up the chorus the main act is on
Deaf blind pianist bursts into song

The district heating which fuels our homes from the heat of burning rubbish is not always reliable. There are often gaps in the service, usually for a matter of hours but a few times it has been days. The worst of these times are when it is winter. The heating was once off for ten days during winter. This was made worse because they don't work on Sundays. Usually the washing gets dried over radiators, but on this occasion I put a line up from one end of my home to the other. It still took over a day to dry with the electric fan heater on full blast all the time. We got a small payment to cover the extra electric and the statutory element in the rent was recovered. Still, it was a hassle.

So, how do I view my home, my position in life and society? I like to think of myself being tucked away in a type of cocoon. As I exist in my concrete box among many boxes I sit and I learn. I become more than what I was before I entered this world. I felt I had not had a particularly privileged up bringing but compared to a lot of things I came to see and experience I decided to change my opinion of this. OK, I wasn't the benefactor of huge estates and money but I did have a garden, shelter from nasty types and I had peace and quiet. Here none of that was apparent. Now that the entire estate is being "regenerated" and I see all around me the continuation of building works I feel like the place itself is also undergoing the metamorphosis I mentioned about myself earlier. The energy of this transformation of the physical can only act to assist my spiritual and mental transformation.

As I sit amongst the tools for making
Upon my fated dwelling of future and past
Never the less I realise a power
Regenerating, creating, mixing and rebuilding
Some silently wonder why the sky is littered
With pylons and cables, wires to hold up the air

Trundling busy bodies in and out of doors
Sleeping in a country house far from it all
But the sky here is polluted with the scent of reform
Make more mess to tidy a mess already there
Pulling out greying hairs one by one by three

Oh it's tomorrow
Oh it's the setting sun
-we will follow
Till the journey is done
I see blue skies
I can see clear skies
And I know you're right
Sometimes
And I know you're alright
Sometimes
Soon it's forever
Soon the days will be
Our moon turning over
Forever reverse the sea
I see blue skies
I can see clear skies
And I know you're right
Sometimes

The site on which the estate was built was once an inner city slum where many people all lived crammed into one lower floor street system. What we have now is the same thing but it goes up. The phrase "Streets in the Sky" was coined for this (then) modern system of housing. The selling point at the time was that each property comes with running water. At the time this was new and exciting, but now it comes as standard pretty much in every property in England.

As I watch the people come and go, I wonder to myself what things get left behind. What would we find if we scraped off the surface and had a look? There are a lot of ghosts around here, how far does the history go?

Spill the words of Celtic verse
Some worldly prose sung unearthed
To a few silent souls in grief
Secret truths from some universe
Scored by string echoed by verse
Giving life to those who believe
Stifling heat of netherworlds
Stinging the skin beyond my words
When none relate with my mind
Undoing time this life space folds
Heat now reduced to bittering cold
An ear I yearn to find

So, what is it like when something goes wrong with your home? The first thing we do is call the system and report a repair job. We are given a day and either am or pm. If you go to work, like many do, then this really isn't helpful. When they eventually turn up, they sometimes gently knock. The way the flats are set out means that most people have their front door on a different level to their living room. Some go up and some go down. This links all the homes in a kind of criss-cross network. If anyone gently knocks, it goes unheard. It may just be because I'm a man, young and quiet, but when the workmen finally get let through the door they waltz in with all sorts of colourful language and posture. For an example I'll mention the time a window was smashed. The guy turned up and ripped my curtain from the wall, which broke it beyond repair.

When seeing the wooden bars over the window (something all flats have on here) he moaned and said I'd have to unscrew them first. I did this while he muttered and tutted to himself. He then smashed the remaining glass all over the place and hammered a piece of thin board over the empty frame. A week later another man came who fitted the pane. In the process he ripped my wind chime down and it smashed on the floor. He then said "I f***ing hate those things". After seeing my physics degree course work he then started asking me questions on the nature of light! So I kindly obliged and opened his eyes to the quantum and wave models of light, explaining why you only see reflected light hitting your eye. It took some time, but after shattering my wind chime I wasn't letting him leave without learning something.

I briefly mentioned drugs at the beginning, and how I had been offered them on several occasions. It was not uncommon in the pre building site days to see someone who had taken heroin or crack. Heroin in particular leaves an impression on your face which if you know it you will always see it in a user. Their eyes adopt a soul less gaze and the skin becomes like that of a wax manikin. I saw one man sat in a piss stained corner of concrete with his trousers down and a needle sticking from his thigh. When seeing me I caught his dead eye stare and he attempted to cover up what he was doing. The sun was setting behind what I saw, and although my compassion leaps out for him and all of his co-users, I did nothing but write this.

Swollen star burns slowly in the bleakest sky tonight
Fallen wings bloodied lie still beating without flight
Crimson waters overflow the sadness carried by a voice
The unfortunate truth stings again I know you had a choice
I don't know what is missing here
I don't know how to dream
I don't know what I'm holding near
I don't know what it means
Sinking skyline collapsing heaven beauty crumbles down
Broken people shaking staring weeping all around
Carried on a cold wind a sigh of a dying infinity
Embraced by cold hands our world lacks divinity
Illness in your eyes I see the lack of empathic thought
Closed to the pain sheering reality cutting time short
Nothing begat nothing the sequence is almost complete
And you choose to stay a while and witness our defeat

The community spirit here is something to be admired. An example I can give is when I had an expensive package delivered. It went to the wrong door. I was none the wiser, then late at night I got a knock. Someone I know from here came bearing the box. It had gone to the flat directly upstairs. I'm quite sure this person doesn't live in that flat, so how he got my parcel is a mystery. The tenants association often put on events for the residents, which help bring them closer together.

Something quite remarkable happens when an event occurs. People come out of their doors and all stand together. Often when standing in silence, conversations will spring forth from various groups which spread around like a flame. Strangers of yesterday are embraced by words which results in future nodding and smiles which before would not have happened. One such annual get together is the fireworks night. A semi-large demonstration of pyrotechnics was given to the tenants for free. Recently this has stopped, maybe the dreaded COSHH or money, but I'm sure there is a reason. During the fireworks period and generally the entire of November the kids play war games. By firing rockets from drainpipes along the landings, they managed to reproduce some tense battle scenes. On a number of evening walks I have been forced to jump out of the path of a marauding projectile.

I was once with a group of friends waiting for a lift. Suddenly a small object fell to the floor from the stairwell above. It was sparking and jumping about. I shouted to run, and we all did. Only when we had just got around the corner, it exploded loudly sending bits everywhere. Scary stuff, but if you provide these things in shops without the need for a licence what do you expect?

I mentioned ghosts of the past. To be honest I don't know what I mean either but there are energies all around me from people who have left their immortal imprints in the area. The sky and the flats themselves are sometimes alive with brilliant vibes and energy. They have their unique 'colours' and 'tones' as would the sound of a flute or the sensation of nostalgia. I have used these to aid myself in healing, spoken with the memories and unfinished deeds. It helps to embrace these things rather than to fear them.

Here I sit in my empty room
And I can't believe that I'm with you
What do I say?
What can I do?
I never knew I needed you
In my life
Again I'm here in my mind's eye
I sense your words and feel your life
Unlocking the door push it aside
Take a breath and peer inside
A sequence of events to shape the past
The spiders will come but the memories last
Just another day in the line of unknown
Step outside and the seeds are sown
I believe in fairy tales
These mythical things are true
I believe in crystal beams
And I will always believe in you

Displaced energies fall into their place
Realigning foci to reveal the inner face
The colours separate and diffuse into the sky
The eternal light that is you never destined to die

So I at this point am still waiting for the work to finish and then the council will move to my flat and get me to move out so this too can be regenerated. It was supposed to happen in 2005/6 but it is now 2010 and still no date has been given. This recession rubbish is the excuse for this. It's just so people with loads of money can sit on it a while and pretend it's all disappeared. Honestly! We have seen everyone else get moved off and seen them given a few grand in compensation, and we eagerly awaited our turn. I sincerely hope that they don't forget about us, the last few, living on a practical building site, putting up with daily lorries and loud mouth workmen. So as I wait, I imagine what the future holds for this site. The energy of the surrounding earth has the chance to choose for itself what happens. It can invite happy times with people moving up and up, or it can remain stagnant and suck the life from those who let their guard down.

Unfair maiden I look upon
thee
Lady unlucky I have to follow
me
Blow on weighted dice
Their permanent lie
But which one knows
What the other will hide
Outstanding unnatural beauty
burn
Crippled spines they twist
and turn
Earth's invisible fluid
Our life running through it
Disjointed our conscious
The leaves of a fern
See a dream in shining clouds
Evaporate into form
See all things that gleam so
proud

And spontaneous dawn
Echoes of the sun forecast a
time
Of shifting and of change
All rivers now one wandering
line
Will never be the same
Fictional crystal reborn
As a sapling at your door
Waters still as the roots take
hold
In the trodden floor
Bell of clarity pierce the
silence
With your simple song
Thinnest air breath as an icy
ocean
Slowly comes undone

I have vastly improved in my ability to be a human being over the past few years, when I decided to take it by the horns I took self governed cognitive approaches towards my problems. This means retraining my mind to deal with things in a way which I deem acceptable, reducing panic, reducing stress and reducing unhappiness. It is a lifelong process.

Oh how their grief stricken faces haunt my very eyes
Neath the satin moon tears are split over blood thicked with clay
Angelic weeping cream maiden knelt before her eternal demise
Swift yet slow the severance withheld while onlookers pray
Just as the pages are turned again

And your dreams are of sun and rain
It's true so many wish the best for your days
And the happiness is written on your face
Things maybe hard sometimes but that's ok
Because you're good enough to blow 'em all away

One of my favourite local locations is the Claywood Cholera Monument Gardens. It is a small park with a wooded area. I am not sure of the history of the woods, but they tell me they are very old and are a small pocket of what used to span the entire hill line. The grand title of the park is due to the fact that a monument was erected to remember the fallen victims of Cholera in the late 1800s in Sheffield. There is a crypt which rumour has it contains the bodies of the dead.

Sleeping souls amongst twisted bracken and stone
A century passed since their minds went back home
Yet their legacy lives within an orchard of woes to walk
And enjoy and imagine their lives hear how they talk
The ivy that mantles the inscription blurs grim fact
To create a garden to celebrate some sad times had
And the fruits bear the signature of vessels long vacated
The names tell a sorry tale all much loved and related
Some young some old but most too soon as is now
A place to walk a place to exist to be happy somehow

As I have been here for over a decade, I have had several friends locally who have come and go. This is especially true as the central location attracts people from all sides of the city. I'm easy to get to for all. Mainly they are nameless and those I do remember their names I shan't repeat them here. Each person was unique and although sometimes a handful would prove to be corrupt in ways I couldn't stand by either being filthy, deliberately stupid or just plain nasty, each person also was good to have around, showed me things about myself which were vital for the future.

As the estate has been well publicised over recent years, for its architectural and social importance, hundreds of people have decided to visit the place and take photographs. I chuckle to myself as people try to conceal their things as I walk past them in the street, they must think I would steal their camera. Students often turn up from one of our universities and write notes and take pictures. They sometimes interview residents and workmen too. I have even been asked what I thought was wrong with the estate. I just said "the idiots". People from all leagues of media have been here. Some even carry expensive video camera set ups and make films, even a couple of entire film crews have been here that I have noticed, to make scenes for bigger releases. Some famous actors have been here to do scenes. From being a dumping ground for social down and outs needing a quick housing fix, to international interest Park Hill has been in and out of the news for its entire 55 year life span to date. My veranda is directly above a yard and I can easily hear what people say when sitting in my secluded but very open spot. When among themselves visitors often complain about the site, the people and the fact they are even here.

Each a glimmer of light to illuminate the path
Each a jewel whose shine will always last
It's all true every last emotion inside
It's all for you as a crystal in your mind
Touch the stars with everlasting arms
Touch the stars with me
Universal pure ethereal before
It's there for us you'll see
Footprints on the shore
Every year I'm joined by more
Shadows in the sun
For once even I was one
A tale of treasure a tale of the sun
A fraction of our realm we have become
A tale of fantasy of foreign lands
A story book with empty pages
The pen is in your hand
Open minded wanderer
Tearing pages from the past
Live minded observer
Making memories that last
Take a step in the right direction
Drop your bags and take my hand
Find a cure for this soul infection
To taste the air is to understand
A ghost in your iris, A message in your eyes
A secret in your goodnight kiss
An answer without lie
A taste of your freedom remains on your lips
The smell of clean air on your finger tips
Gone is the sunshine given in to rain
Dying daylight shimmers on your window pane, far from here

Bearing in mind the context of the last poem, this was written in 2005 at the same time. This one however concerns the events in the news that year.

Unjustly stripped of all they held true
Forced to uproot from where they all grew
Can't live side by side
No sense of community
Opinions cast to one side
For the sake of policy
In our world we respect our own
Whoever you are there's no angry tone
But not far from here
Differences are wrong
People lie in fear
Because of where they're from
So to quench a fire we remove fuel
One man is unable to strike a duel
Taken from your home, for ancestries' sake
Nowhere to call your own, a new life you will make

So what of the present day? These stories mainly have been set in former days when the estate was full to bursting with all walks of life. In those days the noise was sometimes unbearable. From the roaring of a skateboard rattling the landing above the living room like the metallic scratching on the lid of a giant box that you are sitting in, to the shouting of angered people next door or outside. Cars screaming as they speed off from one of the many car parks dotted about.

At half past eleven at night the pubs would all expel their customers into the corridors meaning this was a bad time to go for a walk. I never ventured into one of these pubs apart from once when luckily it was next to empty but I did feel a bit like a stranger walking into a typical Wild West saloon. Well these days it's very quiet. Ok there are still the odd shouts from drunken arguments, or children playing out until midnight during the warmer months, but nothing like before. This secret corner of inner city Sheffield is like a small slice of suburbia. Some amazing art has been put up around the place, on old walls and structures.

Apart from the unlicensed graffiti which springs up all the time, Gary Hindley has made some incredible abstract portraits on huge panels depicting faces in bright and imaginative colours. Another local artist named Kid Acne has written some catchy slogans which symbolize the mood of the area on a few surrounding walls in his massive eye catching style. People actually seem happy, and only the youths from other places still think there is something ghetto about it. It's not like that at all; any resident will tell you that. In fact, the most disturbing thing I can think of is the noise the workmen make in the morning.

Clanging and banging, shouting and swearing, their door is right beneath my flat and it makes a right racket! At about 7am every weekday it screeches open at a snail's pace accompanied by the jolly Yorkshire voices of men at work. At least I have someone to clean up outside my door everyday, who else gets that? Having said this there are still a few hidden problems. I notice drugs still on the estate but I don't think we could ever get rid of this problem totally. Only today, as I was planning my speech on the idyllic-ness of the estate for this book did I witness a woman dangling a bag on a cotton thread from an upper floor window. A nice looking young woman was on the ground fiddling about with the bag, then I heard someone shout – "Just give me the f***ing heroin!"

People still congregate on the landings, mainly those from other parts of the city. People who think it's cool to be seen in one of the quietest parts of inner Sheffield, only with a reputation that is ten years out of date. The locals they stand with are always polite and courteous towards me and anyone I may be with. The trees are lush, the grass is green and most doors are open to smiling and friendly people who will tell you they are happy with their home. They will tell you that although they are looking forward to the time to move, no-one particularly wants to go any time soon. So perhaps it is time to close the story, and leave you with a few poems written from near enough recent times, over the past couple of years. Before I do, I want to remind myself, and describe how I almost predicted my ascent from the pits of constant depression and hopelessness I suffered with so frequently in my younger twenties.
I wrote this as a song but was never written to music, I just couldn't capture the magic I wanted at the time. Maybe soon I'll have another go, as the prediction is of something which is now mainly in the past.

A simple tale of a clockwork man
Whose spring got twisted inside
Now as a statue he still stands
And it's cold and wet outside
Along came a girl one day
Who fixed the man with a song
Magic words he heard her say
That pulled the spring undone
A turn of the key
Try it and see
I'll dance to your magic song
Broken I've been
Many things I have seen

Motionless for so long
She smiled behind long silken hair
Took his hand a gift of warmth
His eyes moved up to her stare
The blank pages have all been torn
Stars are falling as they enter a dance
Flowing to the Earth's natural heart
Each others arms deep in a trance
A clockwork man, a work of art

And here we are, I've told a few stories that help explain what it is truly like for me to live here, and what has inspired the poems I have written. Maybe you now know a little more about the life and mind of one person out of so very many who called this place home, and still do. I hope that the randomness to some of my thoughts and writings just goes to show you how very typically human I am, perhaps a little over honest in places but this wouldn't be a good account if I held back. I have enjoyed compiling this snippet of time and I hope you have enjoyed sharing it with me. I will now include a few bits and pieces that perhaps have no real story to tell, or don't necessarily need one.

What it is that makes a day
As the day I found you
What it is that makes a day
As when I suddenly knew
The illusion of the Suns path
That still traces its line in the
sky
The illusion of the calendar

That defines the man made
passage of time
(Clouding up our minds)
It seems to me
That life is but one day
It seems to be
That nothing will ever change
But a little solar geography
A little more in our memory
And yet it is all the same
And the end of the day

The light I know it's coming soon
Tonight we become the moon
So feel my eyes feel my pupils inhaling your air
And touch the sky with colours of cosmic hair
Oh the sparks alight our way too
They live within us me and you
I know its peace inside
With you as an angel of my mind

The stars they shine forth
And I can feel their light
The stars they shine forth
And tear away the night
Our vibrations reach new
heights
So I can feel your star
No need for pretend lights

Bright universe in each of our
hearts
Oh the angels undergo our
journeys too
They live within us me and
you
Radiate pure eternal light
So we can see the colours of
your life

The grass grows tall on dandelion hill
Petals of yellow and white standing still
The spirit of land is spilling dew tears
For the shards of glass on dandelion hill

Another lost soul sleeps by the wind side
Neath a tree that stretches the old road
No way can this wanderer forget it and hide
For his methods are sound when out on his own

Be gone from the fields now winter is strong
Nothing can stop the onset of the song
Again the sleeper awakes from the spell
A dream now gone where no-one can tell

Outside The Box

A second chapter, from the time of writing until the time I left the building.

Writing this book has been an incredibly important factor in my life since. It propelled me into minor local celebrity status, albeit for a moment or two. I have since written more poetry inspired by these iconic flats, taken more photographs and discovered/experienced many more stories to tell. It has been a long thirteen years since I first entered the boundary, and became a resident of this infamous building. Park Hill has made me something very unique. It has shaped me in so many ways, ways I couldn't have possibly realised, and many I most probably still do not. I am a far stretch from the shy and quiet little boy in grown-ups clothes who moved into my first flat with a group of friends in the previous millennium.

That's right, it was 1999. I am now a single parent of two amazing children, a performing solo singer songwriter, a performing poet and a self published author of many titles. You may notice a change in style from the previous book to this new piece. Two years have flown by since this time. An awful lot has happened in my life in those two years, many personal ups and downs, professional ones, and leaps of faith at every turn. I am enjoying the journey, although no journey is complete without its darkness and periods of feeling lost. It is those times that make the path even clearer. I have met so many varied and fascinating people.

There are tenants here who have been here their whole lives, and there are tenants here who have been here for the whole life of Park Hill. I have spoken to people who remember walking along builders planks which spanned large gaps in the half built structure to get to their brand new home. I have met people who remember standing in the rain while they queued around the entire block (bear in mind this block is probably a kilometre or two in circumference), just to sign for their key. The feeling of elation to move in on here is a long throw from the feeling of dread I felt when my housing letter came through with the name of the estate chosen for me.

I shall begin with probably the most significant event to happen to me since writing the first edition of this book. The time when I was approached by BBC Radio 4 to give an interview about a famous bridge here, and to read one of my popular poems,

"The I Love You Bridge"

Within a landscape of concrete and other created forms,
A sub suburban sanctuary with rolling cubic lawns,
In coves of homes that peer from oblong fabricated walls,
Are folk with minds and souls breathing in buildings so tall.
Perhaps forgotten or misjudged significance led to time,
People carry on running around their personal pantomime,
And the dreams and lives of people existing up so high,
Can be subconsciously swept so casually aside.
When circumstance dictates and you walk through the lanes,
And you catch yourself straining at the highest window panes,
Perhaps you quietly ask yourself "How do they live like this",
Then out of nowhere the answer
"I love you"
scrawled on the highest bridge.

I agreed to an interview regarding the first edition of 'A Poet, On Park Hill?' and when it finally took place, it was a bright and early morning. Wide open blue skies framed the setting as I and the two women took a stroll around the grounds of my home. The tranquillity was disturbed by the council care takers who had decided that the lawns needed mowing at that very moment. The chuntering of motors seemed inescapable but we managed to find our way to a small secluded spot amongst the disused section of the flats.

As tall concrete walls loomed over all four sides of our position I began to discuss with them the ups and downs of what it was like to live here. Along with information about day to day living I was asked to describe some of the wildlife I noticed around. This was a well known setting for me, I often take my children to this little hidden field to sit in the peace and quiet. I tried to really open up about how I feel and what I remember. The things that leapt to mind were, to me, so basic and everyday things, but by looking at the facial expressions of the intent listeners I knew I could just carry on this path. By simply describing in detail the ins and outs of my life at home on Park Hill I managed to capture the imagination of the interviewers.

Then I was asked to take them to the bridge with the "I Love You" graffiti on it. As a resident I am used to seeing this landmark from behind the metal fencing that is surrounding the building site. It has been around six or seven years since I last ventured into that part of the estate, when the giant fences went up. This time however, we had permission to go onto the site. I continued to chat about life here as we walked past varying things on the way. I mentioned my song "Dandelion Hill" as we walked past the very hill and I described to cacophony the song bird chatter that often swirls around it.

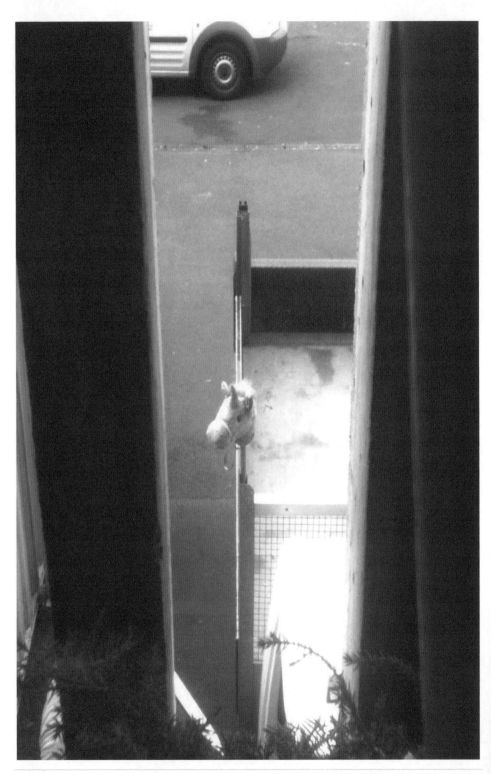

We approached the tall steel fencing, the margin between my home and the domain of the heavy booted workman. My heart twisted slightly as adrenaline crept around my circulatory system as we crossed the border. I, and my two companions marched onward towards the looming and gutted shell of the highest tower. A tall and official looking yellow coated man approached. He held a clip board. Offering us a biro he asked us to sign in to the site and we complied. Once officially accepted onto the building site we were asked to report at the site office and put on some safety gear. It looked like we were going up. After getting sorted out with the right size boots, a hat and a fetching yellow waistcoat we trooped toward the old rickety steel stair. Nostalgia swept over me as I realised I was about to walk up a stairwell I hadn't seen in years. Although now disused, the block of flats the stairs were connected to seemed different but their echoes of life could still be felt. As we walked closer saw that they were totally empty, the hollowness of them was eerie. A few brave souls carrying buckets and things trundled up and down in an orderly fashion. We joined the stair and began to climb. Very quickly, the height began to become apparent. The ground shrank beneath us as each flight of steps was conquered, only to reveal another identical one. Each story had been gutted totally and the bare flats inside reminded me of years gone by. I had once lived in this particular block, the one that was now empty. I was struck at how uniform they all were; concrete boxes all in a row. The stair cases were clinging on to bare white concrete floors. As we counted the flights of stairs, we reached twelve and thirteen, and finally we reached the bridge with the graffiti. I was not the only one to feel an element of nausea and uneasiness by being high up on this spot. The wind was slightly stronger and the ground looked far too far away.

The entirety of Sheffield spanned out in all directions and from side to side the concrete monstrosity carried on this way and that. I continued to reminisce about my life and the things I remember and I also discussed with them the graffiti that famously proclaims love for someone. I also read out loud the two poems about the bridge that I had written, "The I Love You Bridge" and "The Mystery of Claire Middleton". They were both enjoyed and I received some beaming smiles in return for my work.

The Mystery of Claire Middleton

Who are you and what became of your name?
Oh mysterious figure from the graffiti of yesterday,
What was the answer that you so willfully gave?
When yourself recycled a quirk to contemplate,
How does it feel to be scrawled in aged lime?
A name and a question left to the passage of time,
As I am sure that you no doubt realize,
You are a hero of our people, a sight for sore eyes.
I felt important then, as I walked around a building site, as an expert on its history. My yellow hat felt like a crown of succession. I had no idea that I would be doing this, being up there once again after so long. I had walked past this bridge day after day since the giant fences went up and now, because of my hard work, I was accepted to not only walk on the other side of the fence, but also go up and experience the bridge one more time. I am very fortunate.

So once the conversation had become exhausted I decided to take them back down stairs and show them some interesting graffiti on Gilbert Road, the short cobbled track which leads from South Street to the tram lines. I read out some of the lines people had scrawled and a particular poster that someone had pasted up. I read something like, "This is protected as an area of specific urban interest, anyone caught tampering with this graffiti is liable for a fine". Brilliant.

So that was it, my interview was shortly over by this point; I had spent around 2 hours talking and describing. I felt satisfied that by now I had said my piece. We said our goodbyes and agreed to stay in touch, and then I wandered back indoors while my two new friends continued with their research.

When I returned home, I had a long wait before the show was finally aired. It went out in late summer 2011 at 1.30 pm on a Sunday afternoon. That was a prime time slot. When I listened back, I noticed much of what I said was removed, but the last verse of my poem was included. I had a brief section right at the beginning and I was heard describing the dandelions.

Because I am here, and I notice the occasional sightseer with their camera, I often make a point of saying hello, as a way of bringing my book into conversation! As I was putting some rubbish that I had collected from around my home into the back of one of the caretakers trucks (with permission, of course), I noticed two middle aged women wandering around, looking a little lost. I asked if all was well, and with a sturdy Birmingham accent, one replied "Yes, we're fine, thank you". Another case of the shy tourist, I presumed, as those who visit here from elsewhere usually have an unsettled anxiety about the residents here.

However, on my return up the stairs, one stopped me and asked if I lived here. The obvious answer was "Yes, I live there", and I pointed to my blue spring loaded door. The spring load makes the door feel extremely heavy, an illusion, as really inside it is just a hollow rectangle with plywood fascias. A series of questions ensued, about life here, the people, and complements on the surrounding green space and cleanliness. I slipped in reference to my book a number of times, as any good author would, and then answered more questions.

The one I am always asked is "So, are you going to move in at the bottom, where the new flats are?" And as always, I said "No, I want a house with a garden". Like the rest of us, a concrete box in a lattice of many concrete boxes does not seem appealing for a long term family home. Kudos to those who can live in one, I have a large appreciation for life here, I really like it, but I am prepared to give it up to have more room to live.

The new flats on the North flank are looking really smart, and I can quite imagine young professionals wanting to get their hands on a city pad rich with all the modern style fittings. The city views are amazing, and there is something indescribable about the way it feels to live so high up, watching over the valley where the city centre trundles on day and night.

I did have a bone to pick with the design however, some bright spark has decided to lay gravel on the road which leads to the trams, and it's called South Street. This road is a steep hill so the gravel has only one fate- to be washed away into the many crevices and back roads that can be found as you pass from the road and onto the tram bridge. This is not only an utter waste, but also it means when pushing chairs up the hill, such as buggies and wheelchairs, the effort is extreme. It is so much hard work to push wheels through a layer of stones.

The is no pavement, they hadn't thought of that, and when you come to the end of the 200m length of gravel you are met with a fence and a sharp turn to the old sidewalk, cracked and unlevel. Once again it seems that no consideration has been taken for us who live here still.

I always mention this but it had been seven years since we were told we would be moved off "really soon". It had been 18 months time for years. The new build flats finally went on sale in October 2011. Maybe this is what we had been waiting for? Declaration of the final phase occurred on the 14th of May 2012. Will they miss the rent money paid once a week? I have seen a lot of empty houses as I wander around the Sheffield districts, and I'm positive there are enough to re-house us all. The money used to compensate the resident comes from a European body, so I am told, and a vast majority of us are fed up waiting.

It's been over two years since I released this book. Since then a lot of things have happened I'm attempting to recollect all the snippets of historical and gossip gold as I write these very lines. It has come to my attention, partly because of the popularity of my book, that Sheffield and the world cares about this tiny corner of Yorkshire. The hill to the East of town that holds a heavy burden, the hill that props up the brutalist and one of the largest concrete housing structures to form from the 1950's post war Europe, Park Hill Flats.

As the construction work continues in a secretive and ghostly way, marked by the usual handful of workers and the occasional clamour of diggers, some really big changes have happened. The most visible change is the frontage of the largest block; phase one. Some coloured metal panels have been neatly placed over what used to be the old coloured brick work. The modern technique used to colour the metal allows its hue to alter slightly as the sun hits it at different angles. By slightly shifting the emitted wavelength of reflected light depending on the direction in which it came, the illusion of a shifting colour comes to life. It is mainly only effective from a distance and for those of us still here it is not so apparent. By the way, I mentioned those of us still here. It is a well kept secret that Park Hill Flats still houses around 90 residents. I'm sure the rent money from us all each week makes a major contribution to the developers budget, and that this is one of the reasons they have kept us here as they dismantle and fence off everything around us.

To me it feels like there is a considerable lack of respect for us, maybe we are being tarred with the brush of the unspeakable 1980s and 1990s when the area was a crime nightmare and the types of people found wandering around could be quite undesirable. Gone are the days of drug addicts and muggers, they have gone elsewhere. What we have now is a quiet and secluded community in a surprisingly quiet part of central Sheffield. For the past seven years the imminence of being moved off has been there, promises and sugar coated letters. It is emotionally draining knowing that within months you will be asked to leave your home, but months turned into years and it is approaching a decade.

Out of the thousand flats on the estate, the amount actually modernised and ready to be lived in totals four. Now they housing department are saying we will not see removal vans until they first block is ready for people to move in. What they don't seem to realise is that the majority of us don't want to live there, many families here would love to see a nice house with a garden, not a high in the sky concrete box with nice new concrete fixings. Amongst the newly styled zig-zag foxglove gardens with their designer label trees, posh cobble paving and no roadside pavement, the front is beginning to resemble a housing estate once again. The area is becoming quite nice, the surrounding green space and the closeness to town make it a good spot. Crime has fallen dramatically too. They police will patrol regularly and keep potential trouble makers at bay. That is not to say crime doesn't happen, just a couple of weeks ago a man was shot outside the nursery, while children were inside. It's not every day that you see several armed police with automatic weapons patrolling your garden. Apparently the last move in a long standing feud between two rival egos, the event brought quite a crowd. The usual gaggle of residents huddled round, each with their own things to say. The estate manager did a tremendous job with first aid. By applying pressure to the wound with a large towel I'm pretty sure the manual worker saved the man's life. It took over half an hour for the ambulance to arrive, no doubt because the police wanted their soldiers in first. I believe the victim survived and will make a recovery. Someone was arrested but as to the outcome we are all in the dark.

The flats have attracted quite a lot of attention recently. The waves of amateur photographers, students and sightseers all come to take their little piece of history home with them.

We had recently been the venue to two major events, one was the music event hosted by Warp records and one, more recently, was a production by the National Youth Theatre called Slick. It featured loud drumming, lots of singing and shouting, plus acrobats abseiling from the top floors of the building. It was a good show, but I do have mixed feelings. It carried on until nearly 10pm with the noise of hundreds of people, performers and spectators alike. The show itself had 250 people performing it! The noise was terrible. Would you be happy if hundreds of people put on live shows at night while your children are trying to sleep? Again, I feel it is a general lack of respect for us still living here. I and a lot of others feel like some sort of exhibit to be looked at but not treated like people. I would have much rather seen the show performed at more desirable hours, when they would not be disturbing anyone. In the newspaper it stated that our conservative government had slashed the funding for the regeneration of these flats by around 50% Where this left us, I wasn't sure, however the letters stated the moving will begin at the end of the year and I, as always, held them to it. I was actually shocked when the declaration finally occurred. I was eagerly awaiting the finishing touches to the first block, and I am also impatient to see the beginning of the work on the next one along. Hopefully it won't be too long from now.

With steep winding cobbled paths and uneven gorse and shrub covered grassy slopes, this sliver of Sheffield was well used by pedestrians wanting to take a route away from traffic and pavements to their homes on the East side of the city. For years the park remained unchanged, apart from the name, which became Sheaf Valley Park which sounds much more respectable, albeit the artificial embankment that it is, is a good half kilometer from the river Sheaf, which lazily flows on a good walk on the other side of the train station.

As a harbour for suburban wildlife Sheaf Valley Park is in a way unique. With spinneys of Hawthorne, Rowan and Horse Chestnut a variety of sustainable habitats exist there. Crowds of golden and green song birds flock in warmer months and sing while flying from bush to bush. Foxes live in the nooks and crannies provided by years of roots and a steep slope and the small mammals there attract birds of prey who nest in the taller trees. The grass is lined with clumps of daisies and streams of dandelions which add a zest of juicy colour when spring comes round each year.

For years, after the near social demise of the infamous Park Hill flats and surrounding area, this became a near waste land used by heroin addicts and was awash with discarded needles and wrappers. Obvious haunts like hollowed out bushes and heavily graffitied, partially concealed walls were literally carpeted with glistening surgical steel.

In the new millennium the council and generous charities assisted in a giant clean up. Needle exchange vans were a temporary but vital measure and no doubt helped keep new litter to a minimum. Hoards of workers descended on the grassland and scooped up as many items of dangerous litter as they could. It was a valiant effort which paid off. As the flats nearby were near emptied by the council for regeneration the users disappeared and the park became typically clean. It was in 2010 when work begun. The men came with their diggers and machines and they fenced off the most popular part of the hill. The very top is the steepest and boasts splendid cityscape views in many directions. It is awe inspiring and many people had previously come to sit and absorb the scenery. They began by cutting down some trees.

I was heartbroken at this point, I felt it unnecessary. Then the landscaping began. By stripping off the turf layer, removing my beloved dandelions from their hill, they cut out a giant wedge. They also began to produce level sections wand intricate little pathways. Months went past and I began to notice definite method to this seeming madness, and by now they have produced a giant amphitheatre. I could see smart little promenades taking shape and beautiful simplistic landscaping which complements the surroundings. I am being taking in by this.

It looks like this lonely part of forgotten Sheffield may be getting a well deserved injection of culture we could all make use of. In a year or two the grass would be back, and try to stop the dandelions! I for one would be honoured to perform my poetry or songs on the new stage and give something to my beloved community. It took a while but I am beginning to see the virtue in disturbing the tranquillity of my little park.

On September 17th 2011 Park Hill flats saw that injection of much needed culture. The stale and dated landscape scarred with fencing and signs of heavy duty building work saw the official opening of South Street Park, part of the continuing Sheaf Valley Park Network Project. The plan is to make use of all the unused and overlooked green spaces that run along or nearby to the banks of the River Sheaf which flows through South East Sheffield. South Street is the minor road which runs along the front of the infamous estate.

At the furthest point up the hill from the ongoing work by Urban Splash to regenerate these iconic flats the council have ploughed finances into cutting out an amphitheatre complete with giant step like seats with a flat ground area half way up a steep railway embankment. The Super Tram runs at the bottom of the hill which is mirrored with a large brick wall concealing the innards of the Sheffield train station. The first time the amphitheatre was used for the arts had a whole bunch of local performers and musicians.

A music bill dominated by country and western bands was followed by what I consider to the high highlight. A dance group, consisting of local children, took to the stage branding their newly adopted name – "Unique". The two or three dozen youngsters, each wearing a t-shirt showing their name in graffiti style lettering, treated the healthy turn out to a set of complex and energetic dances. Some of the more experienced dancers took lead roles and showed off their tricks and moves while bigger groups repeated well timed patterns behind.

Inner City September Shower

Perspiring heavens collide, with lime and iron entwined,
Forming beaded dribbles of wet, 'pon the walls outside.
Window wide to capture cooling, currents twisting in,
Concrete cages, edifice, weathered walls I'm in.
Pitch perfect hillside, darkness of night walks storm,
Shadow sweeping motorcars, trailing splash filmy form.
Electric lights in orange, reflecting in the asphalt floor,
Mirage of a nether world, backwards in inverted doors.
Desperate and drenched, summer clothed walkers shiver,
Caught by cold, night time world, each pace bringing nearer,
Respite, rest, retirement from desiring home,
Friendly, empty, favoured or alone,
A palace from the pressing rain,
Eye sore but what for,
It's dry, it's warm,
It's my own blue council door.

For those who didn't want to watch the music events that ran throughout the day, there were stalls selling plants and gifts, and one in particular caught my eye. On the far side of the open space, towards the spinney of hawthorn and rowan trees, was a stall run by a group calling themselves 'Friends of Sheaf Valley Park'. They had on display a large collection of panoramic views of the local area, depicted at various stages in history. Some were from hundreds of years ago, and some were more modern. There were quite a few old photographs of Park Hill flats throughout the ages it has stood, an observing giant, waiting for a new lease of life.

At first, when I saw the workers cutting down trees and driving huge machinery into the woods, I was angry. I knew that birds and animals of all kinds dwelled in there and I didn't want my inner city home to be further spoiled by development. Areas of wildlife in these parts of town are to be treasured. But, now the work is done, most of the habitat remains and I'm sure that the ecosystem can recover, if it hasn't already. I saw a kestrel sitting in a horse chestnut tree, which served as a reminder that nature carries on regardless of what we do. I am pleased and excited about this new park, the potential for culture and art is exciting! I hope it gets used regularly, I hope it doesn't become a haunt for drunks and druggies and I hope the council do their bit in maintaining its cleanliness and neatness. I, like many, am looking forward to when the next show is on.

Sheffield is such a dynamic city, every year the face of the city centre is altered somewhat, and each year the people are given a new experience, an ever changing city. The buildings spring up, become part of the scenery and people are attracted, times change, and uses of spaces differ. Park Hill is one of the few standing monuments to the stability of Sheffield. It has over looked this continuously evolving space for over half a century and it is set to stand for another similar period of time, at least.

The people here, I have found, represent a part of this stability. You always know where you stand with my neighbours. You are free to express yourself and so are they. Be confident, offer no excuses and be generous with your smile and everyone is your friend. Mostly.

Brave, Brave City

I was reminded of the hole in
the road that is no longer here

From a message by one of my
friends out there

As a brave boy in a new
shining place

Reminisant of the decade's
previous face

Yet where are the fish in the
tank in the town

Swimming in a cage while
late workers bustle and frown

A street sweeper calls

To a pal from the pub

Whose name is a blur like the
brushes that scrub

Vacuumous tool to remove
yesterday's fuel

A cheery wave and nice
things to say for all

And then came a day when
the city was sick

These days came too soon and
the money was slow and thick

Remember! They say

As they think of yesterday

When neighbours and
deckchairs lined every way

Sunshine in Sheffield had
seemed to have gone

Away

So the southerners came and
put stakes and put claims

Rebuilding the city to mimic
their dreams

A money making frame
supported by rich

So do away with the humour
do away with the quirk

Steel city's on the slab and
commerce can now usurp

The machines and the tax men

Piled in by the score

Apartments and the
Supertram

First busses and steel
contracts for war

Hidden

But think of the class

The smiles and the memories
that cannot last

The soul of the city where
people speak so kind

Now a ghost like the worker

In helmet and shoes

Now we have a soulless
zombie

To find the soul you have to
loose

Clinging on in numbers

Holding on to faith

Deep in the shadows the
Sheffielder still wakes

In the crummy estates

And flats and blocks

Those who remember when
the casbah was the wap

And this is the place

Where the smiles are still
shared

When passing on the rows
These people still care.

When I lived here at first, I did not know anybody, I did not speak to many. I felt threatened and I was threatened, attempted to be mugged and shouted at from landings. This was the norm. I suppose in a way I asked for it by appearing timid, and an easy target. As I have lived in the same flat for the last seven years, I have grown to know those around me. I was staining the whole community with the brush of one or two. Everyone on my landing is really good to know and I appreciate each one of them for their own ways. I have spoken in depth to a few of them and no-one is particularly interested in leaving their name in here, but you all know who you are. I consider all of you equals and friends.

I was awarded priority to move in May 2012, however oddly enough I decided to hang on until the end of summer before I started actively looking for a new home. I wanted to spend more time with the awesome people around me, really get to know them, establish connections and links, so I don't leave anyone behind.

Shed in the Rain

The sparkle of the droplets
As they ripple into pools
The rusted lid of storage
Locked from wanting fools
Hidden tools in the rain
The sun sets over the hills
Potential feels rhythm again
Watched from wetted ground and sills

Directly outside my living room window is a metal shed, the people who live above me have a habit of throwing litter from their window onto this shed. It makes such a noise. When it rains all the bin bags and shards of glass get wet and sparkle in the orange glow of the street light, only then does it resemble some form of aesthetic relevance.

It was early in the year of 2012 when Urban Splash opened the gates to the newly refurbished Park Hill estate in Sheffield, UK. Their long awaited grand opening was attended by leagues of yuppies, generally interested and the quietly curious for a stretch of several days.

A few publications consisting of nothing but photos and occasional state the obvious quotations in large print were handed out, serving only to advertise the flats to anyone who noticed an individual carrying an oversized red pamphlet under arm, spelling out the words 'Park Hill' in trendy and modern style. The run down and decrepit estate famous for crime, drugs and 'down and out'ness has never had it so good.

Well, not since the 1960s when new tenants would queue round the block in the pouring rain for a key to a shiny new flat. Those were the days, when running water and separate bedrooms were luxury. The new owners would have to come up with something a bit fancier than that to encourage the swarms of takers in today's day and age. With the already over saturated market of private city centre apartments, what would make this place any more appealing? I'm sad to say that nothing has been done to make these flats any more modern. On the inside the bare concrete is said to be a 'designer interior', but we all know it to be 'lazy'.

The huge glass sheet that runs down the stair well of the maisonette style flat is just dangerous and a nightmare to keep clean. There is still no room for a washing machine, something that could be forgiven when designed in the 1950s but in the 21st century? That is just plain sloppy. There are nearly 1000 properties on Park Hill. The lowest asking price for a space is £90,000. Many think at this price it just won't work! If each property was rented out the money would be made back in a decade and within two a lot of profit would be there. All this publicity has been a help to us living here still though.

Because the image of Park Hill has had a scrub, and it is almost trendy these days, a lot more people use the main road below the estate to enter the city centre than before. The main fence has been removed and South Street is now totally accessible once more. It was a relief to have that big steel fence removed. And as predicted, the pebbled path is gradually losing its decorative scattering of stone to the tram lines down the hill, and there is still no footpath to walk safely away from cars, vans and lorries approaching the new flats.

I ask you Sheffield, would you not see
These skies of stretching views,
Neat, comforting little mews?
Here, high above the city sounds,
Where light and memory come to town,
And these foxglove lanes lined and paved,
With delicate artisans hands.
Would you not care,
To take in the air,
From an iconic renewal of pride? The face of modernism cannot hide,
Together we walk, together we strive,
This Park Hill dream,
Has now come alive.
Be a part of history,
Breathe life into the past,
Refreshed and renewed,
We build things to last.

As I did two years ago, I wanted to make sure this book was at least garnished with an idyllic image of these iconic flats. I will try, but every single unnerving event courses through my mind as I try to do this. So I shall start with these, and hopefully knit a decent image via these mishaps.

Something I never expected to see was a shooting. However, when returning home from shopping in the city centre, that is what I saw. The actual event had already occurred but I saw the victim lying in his own blood, crying in agony. A crowd of workmen and residents were standing around. One loud mouthed woman was repeating to herself over and over in a decent volume "He's going to die, he's going to die"

Deciding to put a stop to this, I asked how long he had been lying there, "20 minutes" they said. So I thought I'd reassure the poor man and took a good look at him, while one of our caretakers was pressing towels onto his wounds.

"If he's still conscious after twenty minutes, he's not going to die" I said in an equally adequate volume. To be honest I have no medical qualifications, apart from being a member of St. John Ambulance as a child, and I was possibly wrong; however I knew that stress caused by fear was unhelpful. The ambulance arrived shortly after the armed police did. I had never seen an automatic weapon before. The crowds stood back and let the professionals do their work. I was firstly astonished that a man could be shot at close range in front of an active and busy nursery school, but then seeing what our caretaker was doing, risking himself to protect the man who did not live here, I realised the greater good. I wrote a letter to his managers asking for him to be suitably rewarded for his bravery and efforts. I don't know if he was, but he thanked me for the letter so he must have found out it was sent.

Another thing that happened to me, was someone tried to mug me as I walked home. He heard some change jangling in my pocket and was adamant that I was going to give it to him. Of course I did not and the guy became aggressive. I simply walked home. However, after telling my neighbours about the event a group of them went off to look for this mugger to be and teach him a lesson. I didn't ask any further questions. So it became clear to me that day that I was fully inaugurated into the community. For years I felt isolated, alone and afraid. Over the past few years of my life in this area this has changed.

I realised that a smile and a hello is usually enough, and if it isn't then those people are unlikely to have friends either. My pessimistic view of human beings has been greatly challenged. I had every right to fear people, I have endured several awful experiences at the hands of others but I soon learned that unless you were addicted to drugs then you would not be a threat to me, and if you were a quick response in confidence also means I am not threatened. The more hooked you are, the weaker you are. I found this out by standing my ground once and for all.

The majority of people here are normal, peaceful and hard working, and with the regular policing and continual CCTV, it is quite safe. To get into trouble you must start trouble. So keeping your hands clean is the best way to ensure a quiet life. When I first moved in I was timid, scared and shy. I spoke quietly, I was unable to do anything publicly and I would stay locked in my flat. I would venture out once every now and then to do some shopping or to see friends. I would also work nights in kitchens in the city centre.

Now, I am much better, I argue with my neighbours when I feel the need, I have even told some of them off for being rude to my friends. I felt quite safe doing this. Unimaginable! I like it here, I was granted priority to move a few months before I began bidding. I decided to have one last summer here, allow my children to play in the massive well kept gardens and make friends with the other children a little more. I was so desperate to leave before, but I have grown to admire this place. I am pleased to leave, and I deserve the best in life like the next person, but I am also very glad I spent a good decade and then some living here.

Having gotten to know some of the people here, in the final stages of the first era of the Park Hill building; I have learned a few things about its history and culture.
When it was open many years ago, there were features that are no longer here. At the bottom, near the front were public sandpits for children to play in. They were one day filled in after the spread of impetigo. I suppose you cannot chlorinate sand like you would a swimming pool. The old baths, as the pool was known by is now a library. The large brick chimney is still there, disused and reminding Duke Street of times past.

A cinema was here, so I have been told. And Long Henry, the name of the row where I lived, was apparently a real person. Perhaps Long was a name used more frequently in the past. There were artificial caves set into one of the walls near where the nursery is now. These were made of giant piping that lead to nowhere. Perhaps they were used in the construction somehow and were left. These too were filled in, possibly because of the bats. We do get a lot of bats here, and these caves were a popular roosting place, according to those who remember. Someone mentioned a risk of TB, a typical 60s and 70s response to wildlife in the city if you ask me, but there you go. We are in a bit of a time warp here, there are no showers, no room for dishwashers and the 50s design resonates with times past.

There are a few numbers missing in the sequence of doors on my landing. I have always wondered why they decided to make some flats bigger. That is something I am still to find out about. I also want to know more about Linsey and Dyllon (I do wonder about spellings, these were the same two children who wrote 'dumun dum m' on the wall presumably as a reference to the 90s film Dumb and Dumber with Jim Carey). They were two children who wrote their names on my veranda before I moved in. What became of them?

One of my neighbours who shall remain anonymous had become famous for wearing the same pair of shoes for a long time. So, a group of people held him down while someone else went and got one of the pair and promptly set fire to it on the concrete landing. We all had a good laugh at the burning trainer, which by the way began to smell rather funny too, but in a bad way.

I remember year ago, something I didn't write in my first edition but regretted not doing so, I inadvertently became a goon. I once had a friend who named himself after a famous guitarist from Motorhead. This particular musician also shared his name with a famous Scarecrow from TV, and this particular friend of mine was very scruffy looking. I don't want to make a habit of making people look bad, but this guy who I am deliberately not naming was a bully. Anyway, there was this one time when he asked me to come with him to see somebody. I agreed. We knocked on this door that was next door to another friend of mine. A little grey haired man opened the door, nervously and my scarecrow friend and I walked in. This man invited us to sit down so we did.

My companion then said "I hear you've been threatening our friend next door with a machete?" I didn't know what to think at this point. The small grey man said "Yes, but she ..." So my friend, who is well over six foot tall and quite wide, stood up, and gestured me to do so also.

He then said "If I EVER find out that you have even gone close to our friend again we will come round here and break your legs, do you understand?" I just stood there and said nothing. This little man broke down into shakes and tremors, he stammered, "OK I won't, but I wouldn't have used it!" Knowing people like my scarecrow friend has its ups and downs.

It was he that helped me eat everyday by introducing me to the bakery delivery man to the chain of bakeries in town, so in the early hours of the morning we would go down and help ourselves to yesterdays bread products and pork pies, sausage rolls etc. However it was this same man who stole my guitar and demanded twenty five pounds for its safe return. The group of friends I was sitting with while this ransom demand was made did nothing to help. I looked around and said "isn't anyone going to help me?" and everyone looked at the floor. All of them. I paid him the money and then I had to go to his house to get the guitar. I try not to talk to him anymore, although I once saw him drunk out of his skull lying in his own vomit with skin as yellow as a banana. I was really worried.

The friend who was threatened by the machete, who lived next door to the little grey man, that person moved out soon after this because their flat caught fire. I'm not sure why or how, but they were safe. I think they were out at the time. Being on the top floor, the fire brigade had to bring their selves up in a lift or the stairs, hook their hoses to the water supply which was behind locked red metal doors at the end of each landing.

I have seen teenagers climbing the walls of the disused flats and entering one of the balconies. I saw him and a friend squeeze through one of the metal fastenings that had been bent out of shape and enter the disused property. I had no idea what was going on in there, but I know that these kids had homes. Although tempted to follow, I remembered I wasn't in with the gang and would probably be an unwelcome guest. It did however remind me of when I was a teenager and I'd explore disused buildings too. I had a lot of fun. I had visions of an entire community of dodgy characters and strange goings on behind the metal grills, but logic told me it was a bunch of kids sitting in the dark and dreaming of the big time.

You may remember me mentioning a man who once lived next door when I had my bedsit. He used to accuse me of taking heroin, banging and shouting all night long, he used to threaten to kill me, threaten to have me beaten up etc, etc. When I moved, I thought I'd finally got rid of him, but no. Just yesterday, as I was walking home, he passed me in the street.

"You caused me so much misery, you bastard" he said. "I did no such thing" Said I. "I'm going to remind you every time I see you how much of a c**t you are" he said. I walked away. Alan, you must sort out your anger before you get too old to make any friends. Leave me alone. You are not superior to me. I left you anonymous last time but now I have named you. People call you Bobo, you are a character of comedy, I have spoken to many who know you and know how ignorant you are. I have met nobody who has a good word to say.

I have heard of tales involving children in the 70s and 80s whizzing through the freshly mopped frontages on bicycles, and laughing as the women with hair nets would shake their mops and holler various disciplinary remarks. I have witnessed a game of 'tinks' a number of times. This involves throwing a coin at the corner of the wall and the floor, and trying to get it as close to the wall as possible. I believe the coin must bounce from the wall. The closest coin to the wall is the winner. I believe that the winner keeps all the coins. If the coin hits another coin, it 'tinks' and then you keep the coin. There seems to be a lot of keeping of the coins involved so as a novice I decided to decline my invitations to join in. One excuse for sloppy throwing I heard was 'I usually play with pounds, that's why I'm not on target'. I chuckled at this, to think it made him look rich as well as excusable for not being on form.

My final word to whoever finds themselves living in or around the area, passing through, or hearing of it on the media are: Spare a thought for the old concrete, the steel, and the echoes of life. Spare a thought for those thousands and thousands of people put here over the years, some gladly, some bitterly, and spare a thought for the dozen or so jumpers who ended their lives here, and those who died of drug overdoses in their squalid hovels. Spare a kind thought for those who lived here, worked hard, self improved and found peace.

Please, look after the old girl; she deserves a lot of respect.

God Bless Park Hill,
Magnificent,
Sheffield towering,
Sore eyes on high.
To be washed by money and
press,
Reinvented no less,
From the shadows of the
hearts of those who scowl,
Remember the nightmare,
"Park Hill" they howl,
Do you blame the walls? The
lime?
The steel girder that
supported thousands,
Over time?
For the acts of the desperate,

The angry and the ill,
Creative havoc, over spill,
Who allowed such rage in the
first place?
Dumping ground for the
human race,
Who didn't quite fit.
And how do you know?
Who told you about yesterday
here?
The barbeque from a
neighbour, everyone there,
The social support network,
We hold this notion dear,
A friendly face with a hood
on,
That's right,
Yeah, and sometimes they like
to fight, it's fun.